1/27/10

Louisburg Library District No. 1

206 S. Broadway St.

Louisburg, KS 66053

913-837-2217

www.louisburglibrary.org

MARTIAL ARTS
TAE KWON DO

by Tim O'Shei

Reading Consultant:
Barbara J. Fox
Reading Specialist
North Carolina State University

Content Consultant:
Master Robert N. Wheatley
President, United States International
Taekwon-Do Federation
Reno, Nevada

Capstone
press

Mankato, Minnesota

Louisburg Library
Bringing People and Information Together

Blazers is published by Capstone Press,
151 Good Counsel Drive, P.O. Box 669, Mankato, Minnesota 56002.
www.capstonepress.com

Library of Congress Cataloging-in-Publication Data
O'Shei, Tim.
    Tae kwon do / by Tim O'Shei.
    p. cm. — (Blazers. Martial arts)
    Summary: "Discusses the history, techniques, ranks, and competitions of
tae kwon do" — Provided by publisher.
    Includes bibliographical references and index.
    ISBN-13: 978-1-4296-1965-3 (hardcover)
    ISBN-10: 1-4296-1965-1 (hardcover)
    1. Tae kwon do — Juvenile literature. I. Title.
GV1114.9.O84 2009
796.815'3 — dc22
                                           2007052212

Essential content terms are **bold** and are defined on the spread where they first appear.

Editorial Credits
Abby Czeskleba, editor; Ted Williams, designer; Jo Miller, photo researcher;
   Sarah L. Schuette, photo shoot direction; Marcy Morin, scheduler

Photo Credits
All principle photography by Capstone Press/Karon Dubke except:
Alamy/Choice, 5
Corbis/Bettmann, 9
Getty Images Inc./Peter Parks, 25
Zuma Press/ImagineChina/CNS, 26; Panoramic/Ledoyen Benoit, 6

The Capstone Press Photo Studio thanks the members of Lee's Champion
Tae Kwon Do Academy in Mankato, Minnesota, for their assistance with photo
shoots for this book.

1 2 3 4 5 6 13 12 11 10 09 08

TABLE OF CONTENTS

CHAPTER 1
THE BEGINNING OF TAE KWON DO

People practiced **Taekkyon** in Korea hundreds of years ago. They fought in Taekkyon matches that lasted for days.

Taekkyon — a Korean martial art in which people use their hands and feet

Today, people still practice Taekkyon and other martial arts from long ago.

5

A Korean martial art called hapkido uses some of the same punches and kicks as Tae Kwon Do.

In the early 1900s, the Japanese took over Korea. The Japanese wouldn't let people practice Taekkyon. In 1945, Korea broke free from Japan's rule. The Korean martial arts were then mixed together and called Tae Kwon Do.

MARTIAL ARTS FACT

Tae Kwon Do means "the art of kicking and punching."

Tae Kwon Do spread from Korea to the United States in the 1950s and 1960s. U.S. soldiers serving in Korea learned the martial art. When they came home, they brought Tae Kwon Do with them.

Soldiers practiced Tae Kwon Do as part of their training.

CHAPTER 2
PRACTICING TAE KWON DO

Tae Kwon Do fighters wear *dobok*. They also wear safety equipment to protect themselves.

Seventy million people around the world practice Tae Kwon Do.

dobok — the white pants and jacket worn by a Tae Kwon Do fighter

Frustration means you are about to have a breakthrough!

#5

11

Fighters stand up straight and relax their shoulders. They practice kicking while turning and spinning.

Fighters practice their moves at a **dojang**. Tae Kwon Do is full of high-action moves. Fighters use their hands to punch and block. The roundhouse kick is one of the most dangerous moves.

dojang — a Tae Kwon Do school

CHAPTER 3

MASTERING TAE KWON DO

Beginners wear a white belt and have the rank of **gup**. As students learn skills, they earn different colored belts. A *sabum,* or teacher, helps gup students learn new moves.

gup — the rank below black belt; there are 10 gup grades.

A student with a red and black belt has reached the highest gup grade.

Students must finish the gup grades before they can earn a black belt. There are nine black belt degrees. Fighters become masters when they earn their seventh degree black belt.

Frustration means you about to have a breakthrough

19

TAE KWON DO DIAGRAM

CHEST PROTECTOR

BLACK BELT

ROUNDHOUSE KICK

HELMET

DOBOK

21

CHAPTER 4
TAE KWON DO COMPETITIONS

Fighters test their skills in matches. They face off in three rounds. Each round lasts two minutes. Fighters earn one point for every kick or punch to the chest. They earn two points for kicks to the head.

MARTIAL ARTS FACT

Fighters cannot earn points for punches in the face. They also can't earn points for kicks or punches below the waist.

23

Fighters face off at the World Tae Kwon Do Championships every two years. In 2007, South Korea won the world championships.

MARTIAL ARTS FACT

American Steven Lopez won his fourth straight gold medal at the 2007 world championships.

Steven Lopez (in blue) competed at the 2007 World Tae Kwon Do Championships against Jang Chang-ha of Korea.

The top fighters battle for the gold medal at the Olympic Games. The second and third place fighters earn the silver and bronze medals. Tae Kwon Do fans love cheering on their favorite Olympic fighters.

Tae Kwon Do became an Olympic sport in 2000.

ROUNDHOUSE KICK

GLOSSARY

dobok (DOH-bock) — the white pants and jacket worn by a Tae Kwon Do fighter

dojang (DOH-jahng) — a Tae Kwon Do school

gup (GUHP) — the rank below black belt; there are 10 gup grades.

Olympic Games (oh-LIM-pik GAMES) — a competition of many sports events held every four years in a different country; people from around the world compete at the Olympic Games.

roundhouse kick (ROUND-houss KIK) — a kick in which a Tae Kwon Do fighter swings a leg around in half a circle and uses the foot to strike the other fighter in the head

Taekkyon (tay-KEE-ahn) — a Korean martial art in which people use their hands and feet

READ MORE

Buckley, Thomas. *Tae Kwon Do.* Kids' Guides to Martial Arts. Chanhassen, Minn.: Child's World, 2004.

MacAulay, Kelley, and Bobbie Kalman. *Taekwondo In Action.* Sports in Action. New York: Crabtree, 2005.

Park, Yeon Hwan. *Taekwondo For Kids.* Tuttle Martial Arts for Kids. Boston: Tuttle, 2005.

INTERNET SITES

FactHound offers a safe, fun way to find Internet sites related to this book. All of the sites on FactHound have been researched by our staff.

Here's how:
1. Visit *www.facthound.com*
2. Choose your grade level.
3. Type in this book ID **1429619651** for age-appropriate sites. You may also browse subjects by clicking on letters, or by clicking on pictures and words.
4. Click on the **Fetch It** button.

FactHound will fetch the best sites for you!

INDEX